QReads™

Level A

PEARSON
AGS Globe

Shoreview, Minnesota

AMP™ QReads™ is based upon the instructional routine developed by **Elfrieda (Freddy) H. Hiebert** (Ph.D., University of Wisconsin—Madison). Professor Hiebert is Adjunct Professor at the University of California, Berkeley and has been a classroom teacher, university-based teacher, and educator for over 35 years. She has published over 130 research articles and chapters in journals and books on how instruction and materials influence reading acquisition. Professor Hiebert's TExT model for accessible texts has been used to develop widely-used reading programs, including *QuickReads*® and *QuickReads*® *Technology* (Pearson Learning Group).

The publisher wishes to thank the following educators for their helpful comments during the review process for *AMP™ QReads™*. Their assistance has been invaluable:

Shelley Al-Khatib, Teacher, Life Skills, Chippewa Middle School, North Oaks, MN; **Ann Ertl,** ESL Department Lead, Champlin Park High School, Champlin, MN; **Dr. Kathleen Sullivan,** Supervisor, Reading Services Center, Omaha Public Schools, Omaha, NE; **Ryan E. Summers,** Teacher, English, Neelsville Middle School, Germantown, MD.

Acknowledgments appear on page 176, which constitutes an extension of this copyright page.

ISBN-13: 978-0-7652-7637-7
ISBN-10: 0-7652-7637-2

1 2 3 4 5 6 7 8 9 10   11 10 09 08 07

1-800-992-0244
www.agsglobe.com

CONTENTS

Science

Arts and Culture

Social Studies

Literature and Language

Welcome to QReads™!

Please follow these steps for each page of readings:

FIRST READ

1. Read the Fast Facts and think about what you might already know about the topic. Look for two words that are new or difficult. Draw a line under these words.

2. Read the page aloud or silently to yourself. Always include the title at the top of the same page. Take as much time as you need.

3. Find the first page in Building Connections. Write some words or phrases there to help you remember what is important.

SECOND READ

1. Listen and read along silently with your teacher or the audio track.

2. Use the target rate of 1 minute when listening and reading along.

3. Ask yourself, what is one thing to remember? Answer the Key Notes question to help find what is important.

THIRD READ

1. Now, try to read as much of the page as you can within 1 minute.

2. Read silently as you are timed for 1 minute. Read aloud with a partner or your teacher. Circle the last word you read at the end of 1 minute.

3. Write down the number of words you read on the page. Review in your mind what is important to remember.

4. Complete the questions or other reading given by your teacher.

The Five Senses

Your eyes tell you the color, shape, and size of the world around you.

Fast Facts

- Some cells in your eyes let you see in dim light, while others let you see color.

- A blink of an eye lasts about one-tenth of a second.

- A person blinks about 11,500 times a day.

Seeing the World

A car horn honks. Street lights glow. Your five senses help you see, hear, smell, taste, and touch the world around you.[25]

Your eyes tell you the color, shape, and size of things. Light enters a tiny hole in the center of your eye and goes[49] to the back of your eye. There the light lands on a nerve, and the nerve carries a message to your brain. Your brain understands the message and tells you what you see.[82]

KEY NOTES

Seeing the World
What do your five senses do?

_____

_____

The Five Senses

Sound travels to inside the ear.

Fast Facts

- It takes about 5 seconds for sound to travel 1 mile.
- The smallest bones in the body are inside the ear.
- The music in rock concerts is so loud that it can harm your ears.

Hearing the World

A door slams. A cat purrs. Your sense of hearing tells you these things are happening.[19]

Hearing takes place inside the ear. However, before you hear anything, there must be sound. Sound is made[37] when something vibrates. The sound travels through the air and hits your eardrum, which vibrates against three[54] bones. These bones move another part of your ear, which sends messages to your nerves. Then, nerves help the[73] messages travel to your brain, which tells you what you're hearing.[84]

KEY NOTES

Hearing the World
What happens when you hear a sound?

_____

_____

The Five Senses

Smell and taste tell your brain if food is good.

Fast Facts

- Your tongue senses 4 main tastes: sweet, sour, salty, and bitter.

- Your nose has about 25 million cells that sense smells.

- Your tongue has about 10,000 taste buds.

Smelling and Tasting Food

Your nose can smell between 4,000 and 10,000 different odors. Your nose can also help your tongue learn if foods taste good.[26]

When odors pass over the cells in your nose, nerves carry messages to your brain. If your brain thinks a food smells good, it probably tastes good, too.[54]

Next, you put the food into your mouth. The taste buds on your tongue send messages through your nerves to your brain, telling you if the food is good.[83]

KEY NOTES

Smelling and Tasting Food

How do your senses tell you if something is good to eat?

_____

_____

The Five Senses

The sense of touch makes you feel cold all over.

Fast Facts

- More nerves can sense pain than anything else.

- Every inch of your skin has about 200 nerves that can sense pain.

- Your hands and lips have the most nerves.

Touching the World

Your senses of sight, hearing, taste, and smell happen in certain parts of your body. Your fifth sense,[21] touch, happens all over your body. Touch tells you whether something is hot or cold. Touch also protects[39] you from pain. When you feel pain, you move quickly to protect yourself.[52]

Your skin is made up of layers. Many nerves are found in the top layer, close to your skin's surface.[72] There, they can help you learn quickly about the world around you.[84]

KEY NOTES

Touching the World

How is your sense of touch different from your other senses?

_____

_____

The Five Senses

Seeing the World

1. Another good name for "Seeing the World" is _____

    a. "Shapes and Colors."
    b. "How Light Gets to Your Brain."
    c. "How Your Eyes Work."

2. Why did the author write "Seeing the World"? _____

    a. to tell how people see
    b. to tell about the five senses
    c. to tell how seeing and hearing are different

3. How do your eyes work?

_____

_____

_____

Hearing the World

1. This reading is MAINLY about _____

    a. how sound vibrates the air.
    b. how your ears help you hear.
    c. why the brain tells you what you hear.

2. Explain your answer to question 1.

_____

_____

_____

3. What are two ways hearing can help people?

_____

_____

_____

Smelling and Tasting Food

1. What is the main idea of "Smelling and Tasting Food"?

    a. Your sense of taste can tell the difference between many odors.
    b. Your sense of smell keeps you safe.
    c. Your senses of smell and taste work together.

2. What are your taste buds?

_____

_____

_____

3. How do you use your senses of smell and taste when you eat
   a meal?

_____

_____

_____

Touching the World

1. "Touching the World" is MAINLY about _____

    a. how the sense of touch works with your other senses.
    b. how the sense of touch helps you.
    c. where the sense of touch is found in your body.

2. Which is true about your sense of touch?

    a. It helps keep you safe.
    b. It helps you choose foods to eat.
    c. It helps you watch a movie.

3. How does your sense of touch protect you?

_____

_____

_____

message	vibrate	tongue	protect
nerve	travel	odors	layer

1. Choose the word from the word box above that best matches each definition. Write the word on the line below.

A. _____ a part of your mouth that helps you taste food

B. _____ a part of your body that carries messages to your brain

C. _____ a piece of news that is sent to someone or something

D. _____ to keep something or someone from harm

E. _____ one of several thin pieces of something

F. _____ smells

G. _____ to go back and forth very fast

H. _____ to move from one place to another

2. Fill in the blanks in the sentences below. Choose the word from the word box that completes each sentence.

A. Each _____ of the cake tasted different.

B. We plan to _____ from our home to the beach.

C. Juan's _____ told his mother that he would be late for dinner.

D. The flowers had many sweet _____.

E. Pianos make sound when their strings _____.

F. Everyone's _____ has taste buds.

G. A coat will _____ you from the cold by keeping warm air close to you.

H. A _____ in his finger told him that the stove was hot.

The Five Senses

1. Use the idea web to help you remember what you read. In each box, write the main idea of that reading.

Seeing the World

_____

_____

_____

Hearing the World

_____

_____

_____

The Five Senses

Smelling and Tasting Food

_____

_____

_____

Touching the World

_____

_____

_____

2. How can you use your senses of sight and hearing together?

_____

_____

_____

_____

3. How would you explain the five senses to someone who didn't know about them?

_____

_____

_____

_____

4. Which sense do you think is most important? Why?

_____

_____

_____

_____

Stars

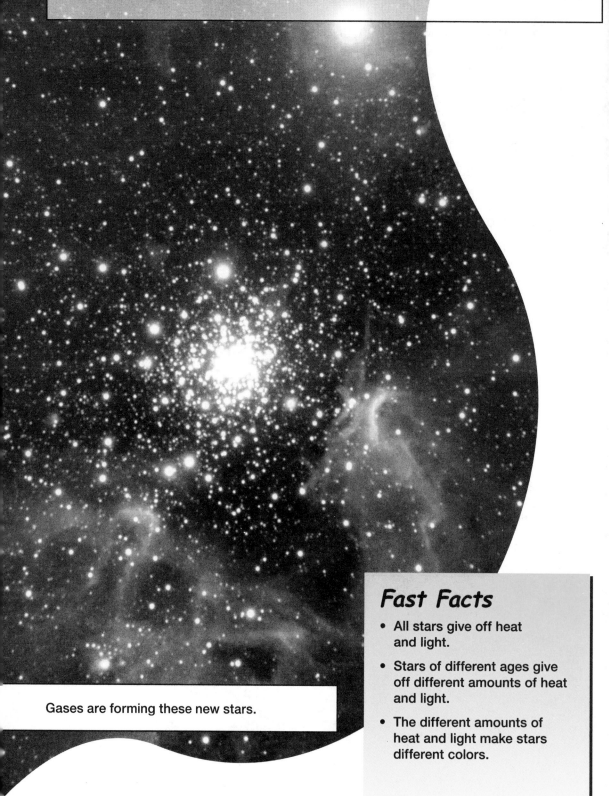

Gases are forming these new stars.

Fast Facts

- All stars give off heat and light.

- Stars of different ages give off different amounts of heat and light.

- The different amounts of heat and light make stars different colors.

What Is a Star?

When the sky gets dark, stars can be seen. Stars are large balls of gas in space. The gas that makes up[26] stars gives off heat and light. The heat and light are the same as the heat and light that the Sun gives off. That is because the Sun is a star.[57]

Stars are much larger than Earth. For example, the Sun is 100 times larger than Earth. In space, there are many stars even larger than the Sun.[84]

KEY NOTES
What Is a Star?   Why is the Sun a star?   _____   _____

Stars

Away from the city, stars in the Milky Way are clear and bright.

Fast Facts

- The North Star is also known as the polestar.

- Some birds use the stars to know where they are while flying at night.

- Near the bright lights of cities, fewer than 100 stars can be seen at night.

Stars at Night

Because the Sun is the nearest star to Earth, it blocks the light of other stars during the day. At night, people[25] can see many of these other stars. On clear and dark nights in North America, some stars can always be seen. One of these stars is the North Star.[54]

To see large numbers of stars, people have to be far from the bright lights of cities. Then, people can see as many as 2,000 stars at night.[82]

KEY NOTES
Stars at Night
Where can people see large numbers of stars?
_____
_____

Stars

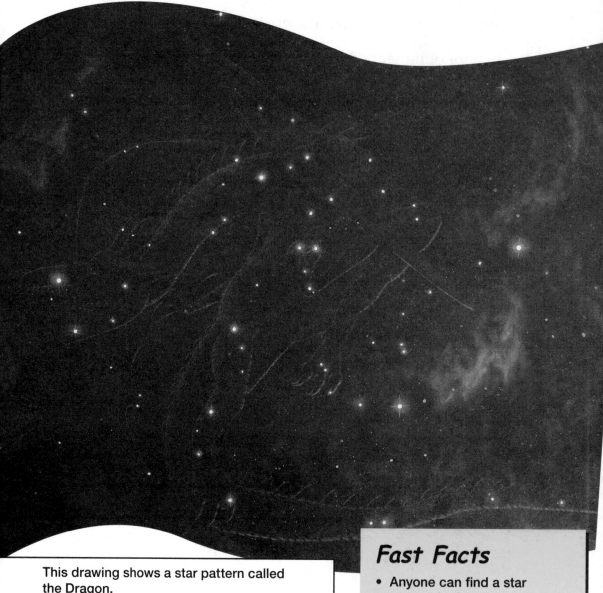

This drawing shows a star pattern called the Dragon.

Fast Facts

- Anyone can find a star pattern in the sky and name it.

- Some star patterns have more than one name. The Great Bear is sometimes called The Wagon.

- Long ago, people on boats found their way across seas using star patterns.

Star Patterns

Long ago, people saw patterns in the stars in the night sky. Many star patterns looked like animals or people. One star pattern looked like a great bear.[30]

People began to tell stories about the star patterns they saw. They told these stories to their children. Their children later told the stories to their own children.[58]

Many of the names that people of long ago gave to these star patterns are still used today. One star pattern is called Great Bear.[83]

KEY NOTES

Star Patterns

How did children learn stories about star patterns?

_____

_____

Stars

A shooting star falls toward Earth.

Fast Facts

- Some people have found space rocks that have hit Earth.

- On a dark and clear night, people can see several shooting stars every hour.

- A star shower happens when as many as 50 rocks fall in an hour.

Shooting Stars

Sometimes it looks like a star is falling very fast in the night sky. People call this a shooting star. However, shooting stars are not stars at all.[30]

What people call a shooting star is really a rock in space that is falling toward Earth. The white line that[51] people see is the space rock as it burns up in the air around Earth. These falling space rocks can be as small as dust or as big as a car.[82]

KEY NOTES

Shooting Stars
In this reading, what does *shooting* mean?

_____

_____

Stars

What Is a Star?

1. What is the Sun?

    a. a ball of light
    b. a ball like Earth
    c. a star

2. What are two things the Sun gives off?

_____

_____

_____

3. Is the Sun larger or smaller than Earth?

_____

_____

_____

Stars at Night

1. "Stars at Night" is MAINLY about _____

    a. why we see stars at night.
    b. why stars are different colors.
    c. why stars are different ages.

2. We see stars at night because the Sun _____

    a. is far away from Earth.
    b. is close to the North Star.
    c. is not blocking the stars' light.

3. Why can't people in the city see large numbers of stars at night?

_____

_____

_____

Star Patterns

1. Another good name for "Star Patterns" is _____

    a. "Why We See Stars."
    b. "Stars That Look Like Bears."
    c. "Stories About Stars."

2. What is a star pattern?

_____

_____

_____

3. Why do you think people name star patterns?

_____

_____

_____

Shooting Stars

1. Shooting stars are really _____

    a. rocks that have hit Earth.
    b. space rocks falling toward Earth.
    c. stars that shoot around in the sky.

2. What is the white line that trails a shooting star?

_____

_____

_____

3. "Shooting Stars" is MAINLY about _____

    a. what shooting stars are made of.
    b. what happens when shooting stars hit Earth.
    c. what shooting stars are.

ago	falling	pattern	shooting

1. Choose the word from the word box above that best matches each definition. Write the word on the line below.

A. _____ a form or shape made by many things

B. _____ before now

C. _____ moving out, over, or across something

D. _____ dropping to a lower place

2. Fill in the blanks in the sentences below. Choose the word from the word box that completes each sentence.

A. The flower _____ on Jamie's shirt made it look like she was wearing a garden.

B. The plane was going so fast, it looked like it was _____ through the air.

C. Long _____, there were no cars or television.

D. On windy days, you can see leaves _____ from the trees to the ground.

Stars

1. Use the idea web to help you remember what you read. In each box, write the main idea of that reading.

What Is a Star?

_____

_____

_____

Stars at Night

_____

_____

_____

Stars

Star Patterns

_____

_____

_____

Shooting Stars

_____

_____

_____

2. What are two facts about stars you learned in these readings?

_____

_____

_____

_____

3. Suppose there was another reading. Do you think it would be about how hot stars are or about rocks on Earth? Why?

_____

_____

_____

_____

4. What do you think life on Earth would be like without the Sun?

_____

_____

_____

_____

Solids, Liquids, and Gases

Heat changes water, a liquid, into steam, a gas.

Fast Facts

- Everything on Earth is made of matter, including people.

- Different forms of matter can be mixed, such as liquid water and solid ice cubes.

- Seawater has two forms of matter: salt (solid matter) and water (liquid matter).

Matter

Everything on Earth is made of matter. Although the air, our hands, and water look different, they are all made of matter.[23]

Although all matter is the same, it can take different forms. Air is matter in the form of gas. Water is matter in liquid form. Hands are matter in solid form.[54]

Matter can change from one form into another. Ice is solid matter that can change into water. Water is liquid matter that can change into ice or steam.[82]

KEY NOTES

Matter
Why do different forms of matter look different?

_____

_____

Solids, Liquids, and Gases

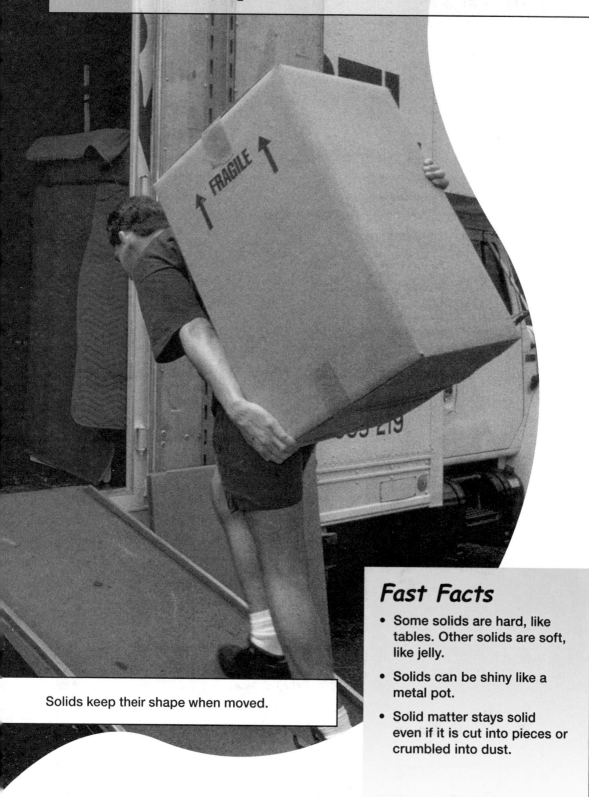

Solids keep their shape when moved.

Fast Facts

- Some solids are hard, like tables. Other solids are soft, like jelly.

- Solids can be shiny like a metal pot.

- Solid matter stays solid even if it is cut into pieces or crumbled into dust.

Solids

Books and chairs are both examples of solid matter. Solids keep their shape, even when they are pushed or[20] pulled. Chairs can be pushed or pulled, but they still look the same.[33]

Solids also stay the same size when they are moved. Books can be moved from big boxes to small boxes, yet they stay the same size.[59]

Heat, however, can change some solids into another form of matter. Ice, for example, turns into a liquid when it is heated.[81]

KEY NOTES

Solids
What is solid matter?

_____

_____

Solids, Liquids, and Gases

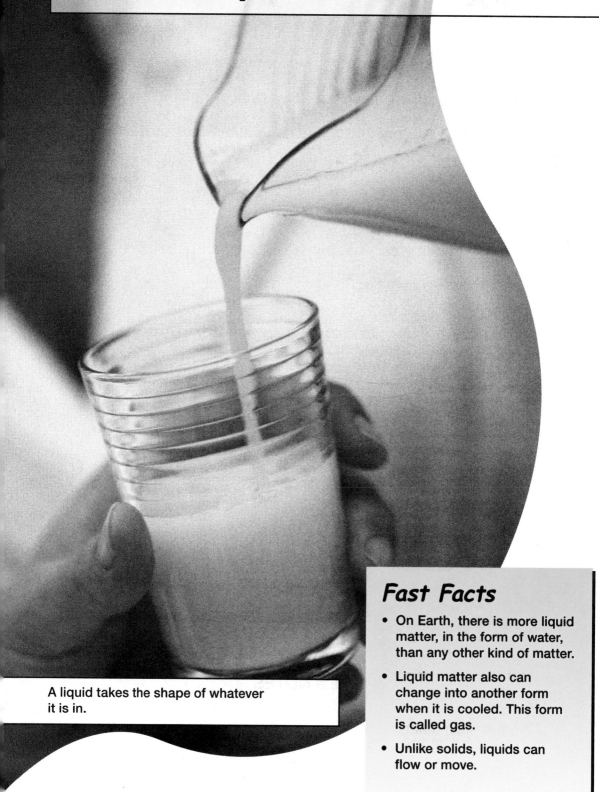

A liquid takes the shape of whatever it is in.

Fast Facts

- On Earth, there is more liquid matter, in the form of water, than any other kind of matter.

- Liquid matter also can change into another form when it is cooled. This form is called gas.

- Unlike solids, liquids can flow or move.

Liquids

Water and milk are matter in liquid form. Liquids take the shape of whatever they are in. If water is in a[23] cup, it takes the shape of the cup. Without a cup, water spills and spreads.[38]

Liquids stay the same size even when they are moved. If water is moved from a large cup to a small cup,[60] there is no less water. If the cup is too small, the water spills over. Heat, however, can turn liquid matter into another form.[84]

KEY NOTES

Liquids
What is liquid matter?

_____

_____

Solids, Liquids, and Gases

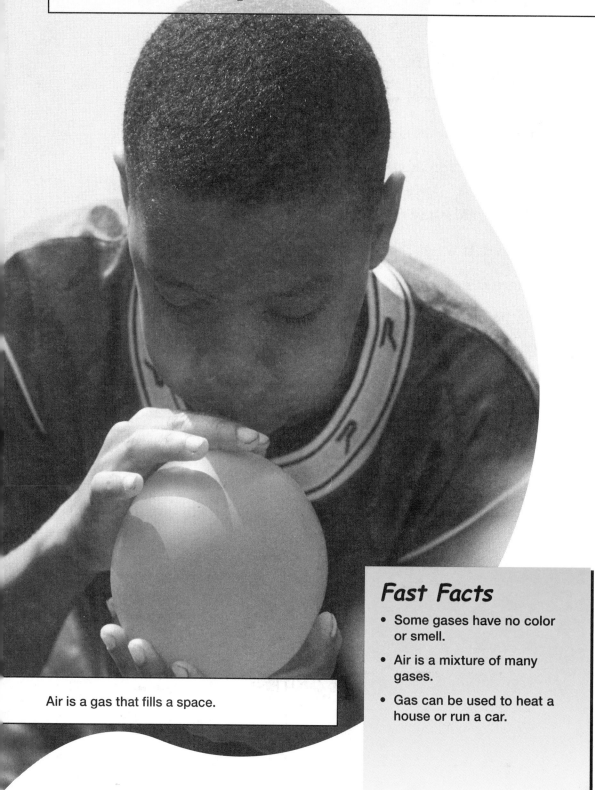

Air is a gas that fills a space.

Fast Facts

- Some gases have no color or smell.

- Air is a mixture of many gases.

- Gas can be used to heat a house or run a car.

Gases

The air around us is matter in gas form. Like liquids, gases take the shape of the container they are in. The air in a ball takes the shape of the ball.[33]

Gases also fill space. If gas is moved from a small container to a large container, it fills the space in the large container.[57]

Like some liquids, some gases change into another form of matter when they are cooled. Steam is a gas that turns into water when it is cooled.[84]

KEY NOTES

Gases
How are gases different from solids and liquids?

_____

_____

Solids, Liquids, and Gases

Matter

1. How are the air, our hands, and water the same?

    a. All can be found in three forms.
    b. All are made of matter.
    c. All are made of solids and liquids.

2. In this reading, *matter* means _____

    a. a form of gas that is only found on Earth.
    b. what everything on Earth is made of.
    c. all of the solids and liquids on Earth.

3. Tell about two forms water can take.

_____

_____

_____

Solids

1. What are two examples of solid matter?

    a. books and chairs
    b. air and people
    c. hands and water

2. How are all solids alike?

_____

_____

_____

3. How can heat change solid matter?

_____

_____

_____

Liquids

1. What are two examples of liquid matter?

    a. ice and water
    b. water and milk
    c. air and water

2. How are all liquids alike?

_____

_____

_____

3. Tell about one way people can change a liquid into another form
of matter.

_____

_____

_____

Gases

1. What happens when gas is moved from one container to another?

    a. The gas takes the shape of water.
    b. The gas changes into another container.
    c. The gas fills the container it is in.

2. How are all gases alike?

_____

_____

_____

3. What would happen to the gas in a ball if the ball had a hole in it?

    a. The gas would stay in the ball.
    b. The gas would move out of the ball.
    c. More gas would go into the ball.

matter	solid	liquid	example
heat	container		

1. Choose the word from the word box above that best matches each definition. Write the word on the line below.

A. _____ something that shows what another thing is like

B. _____ something that holds other things

C. _____ something that can flow like water

D. _____ something that keeps the same shape

E. _____ to make something warm or hot

F. _____ what everything and everyone on Earth is made of

2. Fill in the blanks in the sentences below. Choose the word from the word box that completes each sentence.

A. Land, water, and air are all different forms of _____.

B. Please put the water on the stove and _____ it until it boils.

C. A rock is called a _____ because it doesn't change its shape or size.

D. Rosa needed a big _____ to hold her shoes and boots.

E. The _____ in the glass might spill if you tip it over.

F. Water is one _____ of matter that can take another form.

Solids, Liquids, and Gases

1. Use the idea web to help you remember what you read. In each box, write the main idea of that reading.

Matter

_____

_____

_____

_____

Solids

_____

_____

_____

_____

Solids, Liquids, and Gases

Liquids

_____

_____

_____

_____

Gases

_____

_____

_____

_____

2. Tell how two of the three kinds of matter are alike.

_____

_____

_____

_____

3. Tell how two of the three kinds of matter are different.

_____

_____

_____

_____

4. What forms of matter are part of a glass of fizzy soda?

_____

_____

_____

_____

Drums

Hitting a steel drum makes a loud sound.

Fast Facts

- Some African drums are made with fish skin.

- Kettle drums were once played on the back of horses.

- Today, instead of animal skins, some drums have plastic skins.

Sounds of Drums

People from all around the world have played drums for many hundreds of years. The first drums[20] were made from animal skins that were pulled tight on the drums. People used sticks to beat on the skins.[40]

Different materials make different sounds. Drums made with soft materials, such as animal skins, make[55] soft sounds. Drums made with hard materials, such as steel, make loud sounds.[68]

Hitting a drum makes it shake, or vibrate. The harder a drum is hit, the harder the vibrations and the louder the sound.[91]

KEY NOTES

Sounds of Drums
How does a drum make sound?

_____

_____

Drums

Drums are played during some celebrations.

Fast Facts

- African talking drums tell people about celebrations.

- In some American Indian celebrations, drummers play tricks on dancers to make them miss a beat.

- One Chinese celebration has drumming and dancing from morning through the night.

Drums in Celebrations

People around the world play drums to celebrate important events. In some places, people play drums to[20] celebrate when a baby is born. Other people play drums at events that celebrate when crops are brought[38] in. Some special drums are played at celebrations for kings and queens and other important people.[54]

During some celebrations, people dance to the beat of drums. Drummers tap on drums with their hands,[71] and dancers move quickly to the beat. The sound of drums helps people keep the beat as they dance in celebration.[92]

KEY NOTES

Drums in Celebrations
How are drums used in celebrations?

_____

_____

Drums

Drums were used during wars of the past.

Fast Facts

- During the American Civil War, some drummers were teenagers.

- The idea of marching bands began with soldiers marching to drumbeats.

- During wars, drums have been used to tell soldiers when to wake up and when to go to bed.

Drums in War

Since long ago, drums have been used during wars. Drums were played to scare the enemy. The sound of [22] loud drumbeats made the enemy think it would have to face many soldiers. [35]

During war, drums were also used to give soldiers their orders. The sound of drumbeats told soldiers whether to move ahead or turn back. [59]

Drummers became very important among soldiers. Special clubs were formed to pick drummers who could [74] go to war. Then the drummers had to train for many years before they went to war. [91]

```
KEY NOTES

Drums in War
Why do you think drums were chosen to be used during wars?

_____

_____
```

Drums

This drum kit has drums of different shapes and sizes.

Fast Facts

- The world's fastest drummer can hit a drum 1,247 times in 1 minute.

- The earliest drum kits were put together in the 1800s.

- Some of the instruments in a drum kit have names such as tom-tom and hi-hat.

Drums Today

Today, many drummers play a set of drums called a drum kit. Drummers in rock bands usually play drum[21] kits. A drum kit has several drums of different shapes and sizes as well as other instruments. Each[39] instrument makes a different sound. Instruments in a drum kit are called percussion instruments.[53]

Percussion instruments are struck with a hand, stick, or brush. One drum even has to be played with a[72] foot. Drummers need a lot of skill and speed. Think of trying to hit that many instruments and still keep the beat.[94]

KEY NOTES

Drums Today
Why are drums made in different shapes and sizes?

_____

_____

Drums

Sounds of Drums

1. The "Sounds of Drums" is MAINLY about _____

    a. how to hit a drum.
    b. different sounds that drums make.
    c. the very first drums.

2. In this reading, the word *materials* means _____

    a. things made at home.
    b. what things are made of.
    c. books and papers.

3. How does the material of a drum make a difference in the sound the drum makes?

_____

_____

_____

Drums in Celebrations

1. In this reading, *celebrate* means _____

_____

_____

_____

2. This reading is MAINLY about _____

    a. why drums are played for kings and queens.
    b. how drums are used in celebrations.
    c. the kinds of drums played at dances.

3. Explain your answer to question 2.

_____

_____

_____

Drums in War

1. What is the main idea of "Drums in War"?

    a. Drums tell soldiers when to sleep.
    b. Drums have been used in war for a long time.
    c. Drums are used to scare people.

2. In this reading, *enemy* means _____

    a. someone who is not a friend.
    b. the ruler of a country.
    c. a friend to soldiers.

3. How were drums used in war?

_____

_____

_____

Drums Today

    a. how drummers keep the beat.
    b. the kinds of instruments found in drum kits.
    c. how drums are played today with other instruments.

_____

_____

_____

_____

_____

_____

| materials | celebrate | soldier | vibrate |
| percussion | enemy | event | instruments |

1. Choose the word from the word box above that best matches each definition. Write the word on the line below.

A. _____ to shake or move

B. _____ a special or important time

C. _____ a group an army fights against

D. _____ to take part in a special time

E. _____ objects used to play music

F. _____ something used to make up other things

G. _____ a person in an army

H. _____ instruments that are played by hitting them

2. Fill in the blanks in the sentences below. Choose the word from the word box that completes each sentence.

A. We _____ good times with our family.

B. The _____ was brave as he went to war.

C. Some drums may be made out of hard _____ like steel.

D. The _____ instruments made a very loud sound.

E. The _____ tried to trick us.

F. The drumstick made the drum _____ loudly.

G. Anna plays several _____ in the band.

H. It was a happy _____ for my family.

Drums

1. Use the idea web to help you remember what you read. In each box, write the main idea of that reading.

Sounds of Drums

_____
_____
_____
_____

Drums in Celebrations

_____
_____
_____
_____

Drums

Drums in War

_____
_____
_____
_____

Drums Today

_____
_____
_____
_____

2. What would you tell a friend about drums from what you learned in the readings? Explain your answer.

_____

_____

_____

_____

3. Write a question you would like to ask a drummer about drums.

_____

_____

_____

_____

4. Tell about different ways that people have used drums.

_____

_____

_____

_____

Famous Paintings

The *Mona Lisa* is famous for her smile.

Fast Facts

- The *Mona Lisa* is in the Louvre Museum in France, but the painting was shown in the United States in the 1960s.

- The *Mona Lisa* has been the subject of books, movies, and songs.

- The *Mona Lisa* is worth about $600 million.

The *Mona Lisa*

Looking at paintings can make us think about people we've never met and places and things we've[20] never seen. One painting that's famous around the world is the *Mona Lisa*. It was painted by Leonardo da Vinci about 500 years ago.[44]

The most famous part of the *Mona Lisa* is the woman's smile. Even though she's smiling, she seems to[63] look sad. Leonardo da Vinci made her look this way by making the edges of her mouth seem to fade away. Her[85] famous smile makes people wonder what she was thinking.[94]

KEY NOTES

The *Mona Lisa*
Describe the *Mona Lisa*.

_____

_____

Famous Paintings

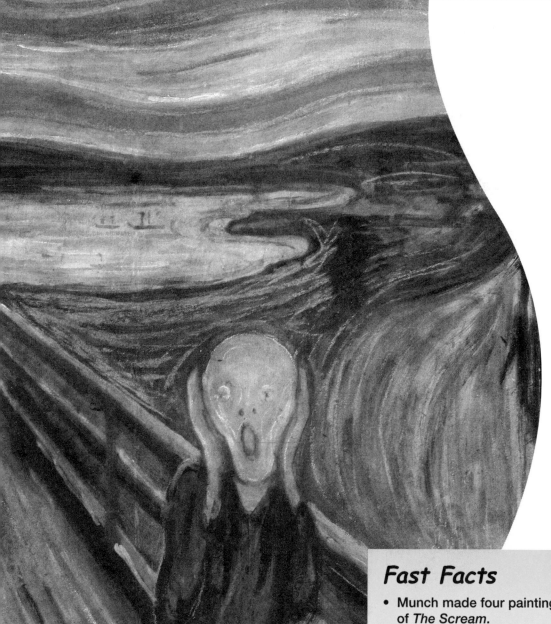

The Scream shows deep feelings.

Fast Facts

- Munch made four paintings of *The Scream*.

- The first painting of *The Scream* was stolen in 2004 and found in 2006.

- During the winter of 1883–1884, dust from Krakatoa, an exploding volcano, caused amazing red sunsets around the world.

The Scream

In *The Scream,* Edvard Munch painted what he saw in his town and what he felt about it. The sky is bright[24] red. A person, with eyes wide open, holds its head and screams. Wavy lines seem to carry the sound of the scream far away.[48]

The sky was red because of dust from a volcano. The volcano dust made bright sunsets around the[66] world. Edvard Munch painted *The Scream* to show how strange the world looked to him. Perhaps he was[84] scared or unhappy and those were the feelings he painted.[94]

KEY NOTES

The Scream
Create another title for *The Scream.* Explain your choice.

_____

_____

Famous Paintings

Van Gogh painted sunflowers in several paintings.

Fast Facts

- Vincent van Gogh sold only one painting during his lifetime.

- In 1987, one of van Gogh's sunflower paintings sold for $40 million.

- Vincent van Gogh signed his paintings with only his first name.

Sunflowers

Some artists show their feelings by painting something that they think is beautiful. They want to[17] capture what they see so that others can see it in the same way. Artist Vincent van Gogh wanted others to see the colors he saw in sunflowers.[45]

Vincent van Gogh painted several *Sunflowers* paintings. In them, he brushed on thick yellow and[60] orange paint to make the flowers look real and bright. Van Gogh painted them in this way to try to capture the way he saw the brightness of their colors.[90]

KEY NOTES

Sunflowers
Why might an artist paint the same subject several times?

_____

_____

Famous Paintings

Monet painted this scene of his own pond.

Fast Facts

- Claude Monet built a pond near his home so he could paint the water lilies that he planted in it.

- Monet made 249 paintings of water lilies.

- Claude Monet was a successful artist but had problems with his eyes.

Water-Lily Pond

While some artists paint what they see, others paint what a scene looks like to them. Artist Claude[21] Monet liked to paint how light changed the way things looked.[32]

Someone who stands near *Water-Lily Pond* sees dabs of paint, not flowers and water. Not until the person[51] stands farther back from the painting does the scene become clear. Then, it becomes possible to see what[69] Claude Monet saw. There are lilies on a pond that seem to blend into one another, shining and changing color in the water and sunlight.[94]

```
KEY NOTES
```

Water-Lily Pond   How does *Water-Lily Pond* look different when a person stands back from it?

_____

_____

Famous Paintings

The *Mona Lisa*

1. Another good name for *"The Mona Lisa"* is _____

    a. "Who Was Leonardo da Vinci?"
    b. "How to Paint Smiles."
    c. "A Famous Painting."

2. Which of the following is true about the *Mona Lisa*?

    a. The smile shows that the woman was sad.
    b. People know what the smile means.
    c. It is a painting made about 500 years ago.

3. Why do you think people like to look at the *Mona Lisa*?

_____

_____

_____

The Scream

1. This reading is MAINLY about _____

    a. a painting that shows feeling.
    b. the fact that red sunsets can be scary.
    c. how artists paint.

2. Explain your answer to question 1.

_____

_____

_____

3. Describe how Edvard Munch might have felt about the sky he saw.

_____

_____

_____

Sunflowers

1. What is the main idea of *"Sunflowers"*?

    a. how to paint sunflowers so they look real
    b. that sunflowers are large flowers
    c. that *Sunflowers* has bright colors and the flowers look real

2. How did the artist paint *Sunflowers* to make the flowers look real?

_____

_____

_____

3. In this reading, *capture* means _____

_____

_____

_____

Water-Lily Pond

1. In this reading, *scene* means _____

    a. the bright colors of a garden.
    b. a certain place.
    c. a garden with flowers.

2. How did the artist paint *Water-Lily Pond*?

    a. He painted slowly.
    b. He painted only at noon.
    c. He dabbed on paint.

3. Why is it a good idea to look at *Water-Lily Pond* from far away?

_____

_____

_____

famous	volcano	Claude Monet	Edvard Munch
Leonardo da Vinci	capture	Vincent van Gogh	scene

1. Choose the word from the word box above that best matches each definition. Write the word on the line below.

A. _____ a painter who painted water and flowers using dabs of paint

B. _____ an opening in the earth

C. _____ the painter of a famous painting of a woman done 500 years ago

D. _____ a certain place

E. _____ to catch or to hold something and show it to someone

F. _____ a painter who painted bright sunflowers

G. _____ well known

H. _____ a painter whose paintings show his feelings

2. Fill in the blanks in the sentences below. Choose the word from the word box that completes each sentence.

A. Five hundred years ago, _____ painted a face that is well known today.

B. _____ painted the flowers that grew in his pond.

C. Dust from the _____ was found in the sky.

D. The bright sunflowers were painted by _____.

E. Did the painter _____ the sad feeling he had?

F. I painted a _____ of a busy town.

G. The painter _____ tried to show his feelings in his paintings.

H. Can you believe that someone stole such a _____ painting?

Famous Paintings

1. Use the idea web to help you remember what you read. In each box, write the main idea of that reading.

The *Mona Lisa*

_____

_____

_____

The *Scream*

_____

_____

_____

Famous Paintings

Sunflowers

_____

_____

_____

Water-Lily Pond

_____

_____

_____

2. Write two things about famous paintings that you did not
know before.

_____

_____

_____

_____

3. Why do some paintings become famous? Explain your answer.

_____

_____

_____

_____

4. What would you tell someone who wanted to learn about
famous paintings?

_____

_____

_____

_____

Outdoor Art

This outdoor sculpture is made from huge iron tubes.

Fast Facts

- In Ohio, a sculpture called Field of Corn has 109 concrete ears of corn, each standing about 6 feet tall.

- The world's tallest sand sculpture, a sand castle, is almost 29 feet high.

- The world's largest ice palace, in Minnesota, had about 20,000 ice blocks.

What Is Outdoor Art?

When you think about looking at art, you might think of going to a museum to see paintings hanging[23] on walls. However, art can also be found outdoors, too. You may have seen big paintings on the outside walls[43] of buildings. These paintings often show people or things that are nearby.[55]

Other kinds of outdoor art can be found in the sculpture gardens of some museums. When sculptures[72] are placed outdoors, people can walk around them and look at them in different ways. Outdoor sculptures can be enjoyed by everyone.[94]

KEY NOTES

What Is Outdoor Art?
Why might someone want to make art to be placed outdoors?

_____

_____

Outdoor Art

The "Jazz Cow" was in Chicago's outdoor art show.

Fast Facts

- Cincinnati had a show of pig sculptures.

- CowParade®, in Chicago, placed 340 cow sculptures around the city.

- In New York City, sculpture cows were sold, and $1.35 million was given to charities.

City Sculptures

Some outdoor sculptures are shaped like animals. In fact, many cities have had public shows of animal[19] sculptures. In these shows, artists have painted sculptures of cows, pigs, horses, and other animals in hundreds of different ways.[39]

People enjoy these sculptures because they show how different artists put their ideas to work. To add to[57] the fun, the sculptures are put in many public places so people can be surprised as they walk through a city.[78] Around the next corner, there could be a cow painted to look like a movie star.[94]

KEY NOTES

City Sculptures

What kinds of animal sculptures have been shown in cities?

_____

_____

Outdoor Art

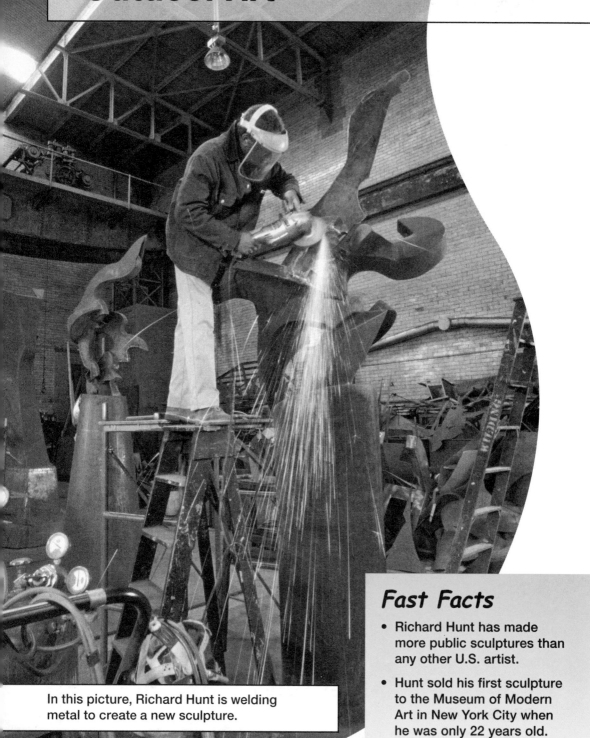

In this picture, Richard Hunt is welding metal to create a new sculpture.

Fast Facts

- Richard Hunt has made more public sculptures than any other U.S. artist.

- Hunt sold his first sculpture to the Museum of Modern Art in New York City when he was only 22 years old.

- Hunt earned $500,000 for a sculpture he made for a fountain in Washington, D.C.

Richard Hunt

Richard Hunt is an artist who makes sculptures. He has made more than 100 outdoor sculptures. Most were[20] made from metal. The top of one of Richard Hunt's sculptures is twisted into wings. Another sculpture[37] looks like a person changing into a bug. The bug's eyes are made from a car's lights.[54]

Hunt builds many of his sculptures from trash. He cuts and shapes metal things that people have thrown[72] out, such as shopping carts and parts from trucks. Richard Hunt is an artist who turns metal trash into art.[92]

KEY NOTES
Richard Hunt
What are some things used in Richard Hunt's art?
_____
_____

Outdoor Art

In 2005, Christo set up an outdoor sculpture in New York City's Central Park.

Fast Facts

- Christo set up a cloth fence that ran for 20 miles.

- Christo put silver cloth around a building.

- Christo set up a chain of umbrellas weighing 485 pounds each.

Temporary Outdoor Art

Most outdoor art is made to last a long time. However, an artist named Christo makes outdoor art[21] that is temporary. What Christo wants to do with his art is to change a setting, but only for a short time.[43]

In 2005, Christo hung pieces of cloth that he called gates, in a New York City park. From far away, the cloth looked like a golden river.[70]

After two weeks, Christo takes down his art because he thinks that temporary art makes people see a setting in a new way.[93]

KEY NOTES

Temporary Outdoor Art

Why do you think most outdoor art is made to last a long time?

_____

_____

Outdoor Art

What Is Outdoor Art?

1. "What Is Outdoor Art?" is MAINLY about _____

    a. art that looks like real things.
    b. art that is outside of buildings.
    c. art that people can walk around.

2. Why did the author write "What Is Outdoor Art?"

    a. to tell about large and small sculptures
    b. to tell about how outdoor art is made
    c. to tell about where to find outdoor art

3. What are two kinds of outdoor art?

_____

_____

_____

City Sculptures

1. In this reading, *public* means _____

    a. animals that are painted in different ways.
    b. something that everyone can do or see.
    c. sculptures that are shown outdoors.

2. This reading is MAINLY about _____

    a. shows of animal sculptures in cities.
    b. how to make cow sculptures.
    c. making sculptures that no one had ever seen before.

3. Explain your answer to question 2.

_____

_____

_____

Richard Hunt

1. Another good name for "Richard Hunt" is _____

    a. "How to Work With Metal."
    b. "The Life of Richard Hunt."
    c. "Turning Trash Into Art."

2. Explain your answer to question 1.

_____

_____

_____

3. Write two facts you learned about Richard Hunt.

_____

_____

_____

Temporary Outdoor Art

1. Which words below have almost the same meaning as *temporary?*

    a. the same
    b. not lasting a long time
    c. very new

2. The main idea of this reading is that _____

    a. all outdoor art is made to last a long time.
    b. outdoor art can be made of cloth.
    c. some outdoor art is not made to last a long time.

3. Why does Christo make temporary art?

_____

_____

_____

sculpture	public	temporary
museum	metal	artists

1. Choose the word from the word box above that best matches each definition. Write the word on the line below.

A. _____ for a short time

B. _____ art that is shaped and can stand on its own

C. _____ people who create art

D. _____ open to everyone

E. _____ a place to see art

F. _____ a hard material that is used to make cars, trucks, and other things

2. Fill in the blanks in the sentences below. Choose the word from the word box that completes each sentence.

A. We plan to visit the _____ to see the new paintings.

B. Manuel shaped paper to make a _____ that looked like a huge bug.

C. Three _____ worked together to paint the huge wall painting.

D. The _____ in the car bent when it hit the pole.

E. The new park was open to the _____.

F. The snow was only a _____ problem because it melted quickly.

Outdoor Art

1. Use the idea web to help you remember what you read. For each reading title, write the main idea of that reading.

What Is Outdoor Art?

_____

_____

_____

_____

City Sculptures

_____

_____

_____

_____

Outdoor Art

Richard Hunt

_____

_____

_____

_____

Temporary Outdoor Art

_____

_____

_____

_____

2. Choose two of the artists or artworks in this topic. Tell how they are alike and different.

_____

_____

_____

_____

3. How are outdoor art and indoor art alike and different?

_____

_____

_____

_____

4. What would you tell someone who wanted to learn about outdoor art?

_____

_____

_____

_____

Americans Who Dream

President Theodore Roosevelt looks at Yosemite National Park in California, before it was a park.

Fast Facts

- Before Theodore Roosevelt became president, he lived in the country and took care of animals.

- The world's first national park was Yellowstone National Park in Wyoming.

- Other countries around the world have nature parks because of Roosevelt's idea.

Theodore Roosevelt

President Theodore Roosevelt believed that nature was an important part of the United States. He believed[18] that people should care for wild animals and plants. President Roosevelt's dream was that nature would always be there to enjoy.[39]

As president, Roosevelt worked for laws to keep natural areas from being used for other things. These[56] laws saved millions of acres of land for use as nature parks. President Roosevelt made sure that there would[75] always be natural areas that everyone in the United States could enjoy. Today, more than 100 years later, millions of people visit these parks each year.[101]

KEY NOTES

Theodore Roosevelt

How did President Roosevelt's dream come true?

_____

_____

Americans Who Dream

Kristi Yamaguchi worked hard to make her dream of ice skating come true.

Fast Facts

- Kristi Yamaguchi was the first Asian American woman to win an Olympic gold medal in any sport.

- Yamaguchi has won many medals in ice skating.

- Yamaguchi started a group that helps children follow their dreams.

Kristi Yamaguchi

As a child, Kristi Yamaguchi dreamed about ice skating in the Olympic Games. She had to work even harder than[22] most people to make that dream come true. That's because one of Yamaguchi's feet had a problem. Her family helped her work to become an Olympic ice skater.[50]

In 1992, Kristi Yamaguchi skated in the Olympics. When her turn to skate came, she fell. Instead of stopping,[69] though, Yamaguchi kept skating. She skated so well that she won the Olympic gold medal as the best woman ice[89] skater in the world. Yamaguchi says, "Just do your very best, and always dream."[103]

KEY NOTES
Kristi Yamaguchi
How did Kristi Yamaguchi's dream come true?
_____
_____

Americans Who Dream

Wilbur and Orville Wright first fly an airplane in 1903.

Fast Facts

- Wilbur was the first to fly the plane the brothers built.

- People gave the Wright brothers money to build more planes.

- The field where the first plane was flown is now in the Wright Brothers National Park in North Carolina.

The Wright Brothers

When Wilbur and Orville Wright were children, they flew kites. At that time, there were no airplanes.[20] However, the Wright brothers dreamed about flying through the air.[30]

After they grew up, the Wright brothers began making an airplane. They faced many problems.[45] At last, though, they made an airplane that could fly. Their airplane flew for only seconds, but the Wright brothers were still the first people to fly.[72]

The brothers' dream led to the airplanes of today. Once people knew they could fly, they dreamed of flying[91] faster and farther. Now, some airplanes fly faster than sound and into space.[104]

KEY NOTES

The Wright Brothers
How did the Wright brothers' dream come true?

_____

_____

Americans Who Dream

Doctor Charles Drew found a new way to keep blood fresh and save many lives.

Fast Facts

- Charles Drew was an All-American football player in school.

- Drew got some money for school by teaching others how to play football.

- Drew helped get people well for the United States army and navy.

Charles Drew

When Charles Drew was young, not many African
Americans were doctors. Charles Drew, who was African[18]
American, did not let this stop him. After high school,
he studied at one of the few schools that took African[39]
American students. He worked hard to find his dream.
He finally became a doctor.[53]

As a doctor, Charles Drew worked hard to find the
answer to an important problem. He found a way to keep[74]
blood fresh. When blood can be kept fresh, it can be used
to make people well. Because of Charles Drew's dream,
millions of lives are saved every year.[102]

KEY NOTES

Charles Drew

How did Charles Drew's dream come true?

_____

_____

Americans Who Dream

Theodore Roosevelt

1. President Theodore Roosevelt worked for laws that _____

    a. made money.
    b. made nature.
    c. made parks.

2. What was President Theodore Roosevelt's dream?

_____

_____

_____

3. How did President Roosevelt save land for nature parks?

_____

_____

_____

Kristi Yamaguchi

1. Another good name for "Kristi Yamaguchi" is _____

    a. "The Olympic Games."
    b. "A Skater's Dream."
    c. "How to Ice Skate."

2. Yamaguchi had to work very hard to skate in the Olympics because _____

    a. she did not believe that she could win.
    b. she fell many times when she skated.
    c. one of her feet had a problem.

3. What was Kristi Yamaguchi's dream?

_____

_____

_____

The Wright Brothers

1. After they grew up, the Wright brothers _____

    a. made an airplane.
    b. flew kites.
    c. made today's airplanes.

2. What was the Wright brothers' dream?

_____

_____

_____

3. How did the Wright brothers' dream lead to the airplanes of today?

_____

_____

_____

Charles Drew

1. Charles Drew's dream was to become _____

    a. a doctor.
    b. a teacher.
    c. a writer.

2. Charles Drew had trouble making his dream come true
because _____

    a. few schools took African American students.
    b. he was too young to go to school to become a doctor.
    c. it was hard for African Americans to have dreams.

3. What was the problem Charles Drew solved?

_____

_____

_____

president	believed	nature	Olympics
skating	airplane	African	doctor

1. Choose the word from the word box above that best matches each definition. Write the word on the line below.

A. _____ all the things in the world that are not made by people

B. _____ thought something was true

C. _____ gliding on ice

D. _____ the leader of a group or a country

E. _____ something that carries people through the air

F. _____ a sports contest that is held every four years

G. _____ a person who helps sick people get well

H. _____ someone or something from Africa

2. Fill in the blanks in the sentences below. Choose the word from the word box that completes each sentence.

A. I went to see a _____ when I got sick.

B. I like to watch the track events at the _____.

C. Many _____ Americans have dreams to become doctors.

D. An _____ flew me across the country to visit my grandmother.

E. I like _____ because it makes me feel like I'm floating on the ice.

F. The leader of the United States is called the _____.

G. Sam _____ that his part-time job would help his family.

H. Rena looks at the flowers when she goes on _____ walks in the park.

Americans Who Dream

1. Use the idea web to help you remember what you read. In each box, write the main idea of that reading.

Theodore Roosevelt

_____

_____

_____

Kristi Yamaguchi

_____

_____

_____

Americans Who Dream

The Wright Brothers

_____

_____

_____

Charles Drew

_____

_____

_____

2. How did two of these people make their dreams come true?

_____

_____

_____

_____

3. Tell about one way all of these people are alike.

_____

_____

_____

_____

4. Is "Never Give Up" a good title for these readings? Explain.

_____

_____

_____

_____

Careers

Salespeople must know the costs of the goods they sell.

Fast Facts

- Some salespeople go to people's homes to sell things.

- Some sales careers involve selling over the telephone, or telemarketing.

- In 2005, about 17 million people in the United States worked in sales.

Choosing a Career

When you think about choosing a career, begin with what interests you. A career is the kind of work that you[24] will do for a long time. So you'll want to choose work that you'll enjoy.[39]

There are many kinds of careers. Many people are interested in sales. They work for places that make things[58] for stores or that sell things to stores. Other salespeople work in stores. Wherever they work, though,[75] salespeople must know about the goods they sell and how much they cost.[88]

Most salespeople work with others. Think about a sales career if you enjoy working with people.[104]

KEY NOTES

Choosing a Career
What should you think about when you're choosing a career?

What interests you. career.

Careers

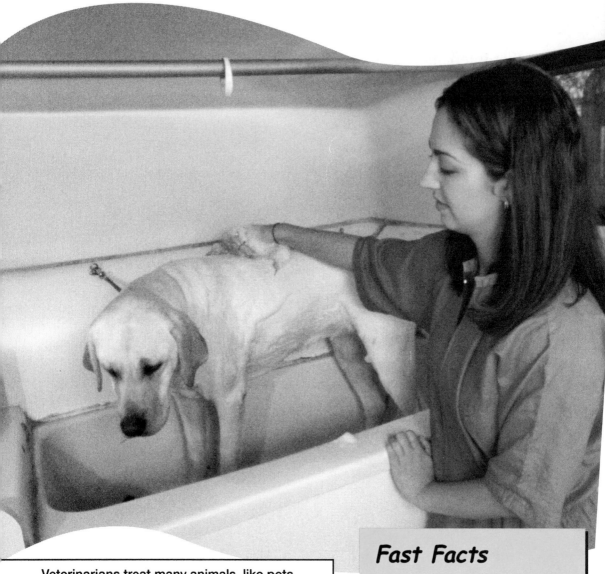

Veterinarians treat many animals, like pets that have skin problems.

Fast Facts

- A vet needs at least four years of training and then must pass a special test in order to treat animals.

- Some vets treat homeless pets in animal shelters.

- One challenge vets face is that animals can't tell them what hurts.

Working with Animals

Many people have careers working with animals. People who choose these careers should like being near[19] animals. One kind of career that helps animals is that of a veterinarian, or vet. A vet is a doctor who treats animals.[42]

A veterinarian must find out what problem an animal has and treat it. Some vets treat only pets that have certain[63] problems, like problems with their skin. Some treat only pets, like dogs, cats, and rabbits, while others treat only[82] large animals, like horses and cows. Some veterinarians also treat only wild animals, like ducks and deer that are sick or hurt.[104]

KEY NOTES

Working with Animals
What kinds of problems do veterinarians treat?

_____

_____

Careers

Music is recorded and mixed in a studio.

Fast Facts

- Some radio stations have ads and other stations get money from listeners.

- Many people work only in recording studios, playing with well-known performers or making commercials or sound tracks.

- Most people with music careers teach music.

Working in Music

Many people have careers in music. Some people compose music for themselves or others to play. Some[20] compose music for movies or TV shows. People also work in places where music is recorded. These people mix[39] music that is being recorded. Still other people sell CDs in music stores.[52]

Some people with music careers work in radio. Radio DJs might choose the music they play and talk to people[72] who make music. To be radio DJs, people have to know about music and the kind of music people want to hear. Then, they can play music people like.[101]

KEY NOTES

Working in Music

What kinds of careers in music could people choose?

_____

_____

Careers

Construction workers are skilled and often work outside.

Fast Facts

- About one-third of all construction workers in the United States are carpenters.

- In 2004, almost 9 million people worked in the U.S. construction trade.

- Construction workers build houses, highways, and bridges, and many other things.

Working in Construction

Many people who enjoy working with their hands and with tools choose careers in the trades. Trade workers[21] do many kinds of skilled work, including constructing buildings, laying down water pipes, and fixing cars.[37]

One kind of career is in the construction trade. Construction workers build or fix homes or highways.[54] Sometimes they have dangerous work, like constructing a bridge above a river. Many construction workers work[70] outside in rain or heat. Because most building is done in months when the weather is warm, construction workers[89] who work outside are sometimes out of work during cold weather.[100]

KEY NOTES

Working in Construction
What kinds of careers in construction could people choose?

_____

_____

Careers

Choosing a Career

1. This reading is MAINLY about _____

    a. how to begin choosing a career.
    b. how to find a job working in sales.
    c. how salespeople work with people.

2. Why should people choose work they'll enjoy?

_____

_____

_____

3. In this reading, *career* means _____

    a. how people find work.
    b. a path to follow during your working life.
    c. a way to make money.

Working with Animals

1. What do veterinarians do in their career?

_____

_____

_____

2. Another good name for "Working With Animals" is _____

    a. "How to Make Sick Animals Well."
    b. "Becoming a Veterinarian."
    c. "A Career in Caring for Animals."

3. Explain your answer to question 2.

_____

_____

_____

Working in Music

1. This reading is MAINLY about _____

    a. why people work in music.
    b. how to become a radio DJ.
    c. different kinds of music careers.

2. Explain your answer to question 1.

_____

_____

_____

3. In this reading, what does *compose* mean?

_____

_____

_____

Working in Construction

1. In this reading, *the trades* means _____

    a. work that people must have certain skills to do.

    b. ways to sell or exchange things.

    c. careers in construction.

2. What are two kinds of things construction workers might build?

_____

_____

_____

3. Why might construction workers be out of work in the winter?

_____

_____

_____

career	interest	veterinarian	treat
compose	record	trade	construction

1. Choose the word from the word box above that best matches each definition. Write the word on the line below.

A. _____ a kind of skilled work that usually involves building or fixing things

B. _____ to create CDs or other music

C. _____ to write something, such as music

D. _____ a path followed during a working life

E. _____ something a person likes to do

F. _____ a doctor who takes care of animals

G. _____ the act of building something

H. _____ to take care of or help something or someone

2. Fill in the blanks in the sentences below. Choose the word from the word box that completes each sentence.

A. Maria wanted to _____ a CD so others could hear her music.

B. The _____ helped the sick cat.

C. Jake's father worked in a _____ in which he fixed cars.

D. Sam got some pills to _____ his sick dog.

E. Maria was asked to _____ a new song for a TV show.

F. The _____ job involved building a new bridge.

G. It is important to know what kinds of things _____ you.

H. I want to have a _____ in the music business.

Careers

1. Use the idea web to help you remember what you read. In each
box, write the main idea of that reading.

Choosing a Career

_____

_____

_____

Working with Animals

_____

_____

_____

Careers

Working in Music

_____

_____

_____

_____

Working in Construction

_____

_____

_____

_____

2. How are two of the careers in this topic alike?

_____

_____

_____

_____

3. How are two of the careers in this topic different?

_____

_____

_____

_____

4. Write a question you would like to ask the writer about careers.

_____

_____

_____

_____

The Stone Age

These cave paintings were made in the Stone Age.

Fast Facts

- The earliest people arrived in North America more than 20,000 years ago.

- The most complete set of Stone-Age bones was found in 1974 in Africa.

- Scientists named this early relative of humans Lucy.

The Earliest People

Although people have been on Earth for a long time, not much is known about the earliest people. That is[23] because no one has found any art or tools that the earliest people made. Studying things like bowls or spears can tell scientists how people lived long ago.[51]

Once people learned to make tools, they made drawings on the walls of caves. They also made bowls[69] and spears. The earliest tools that have been found were made from stones. Because the people from long ago used[89] stones to make tools, scientists have called this time the Stone Age.[101]

KEY NOTES
The Earliest People
How do scientists learn about early people?
_____
_____

The Stone Age

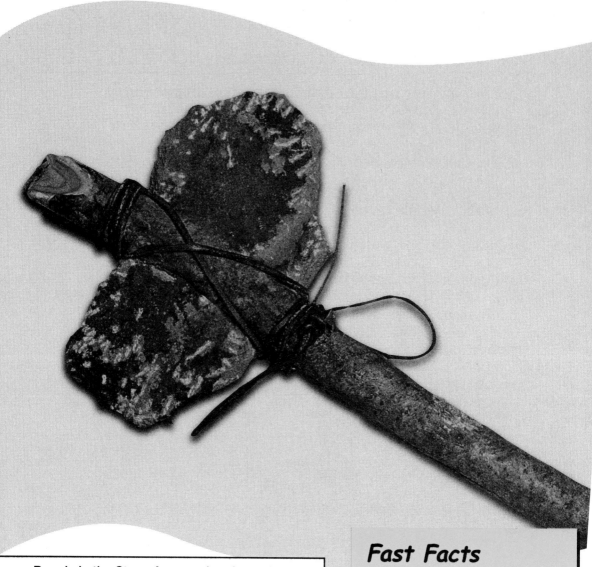

People in the Stone Age used tools made of stone, wood, or bone.

Fast Facts

- The earliest people chipped bone to make tools. Later people smoothed bone when making tools.

- Chimpanzees, like humans, use tools to get food.

- Stone-Age people used tools to make musical instruments, such as flutes.

Tools

The earliest people probably used sticks to get food. Later, people made tools from stones and animal bones.[19] These new tools were stronger and lasted longer than sticks. Stronger tools helped people hunt for animals[36] without getting close to them. People could also catch fish with hooks that they made from animal bones. In this[56] way, bone and stone tools helped early people get more food and stay safe.[70]

Early people also used stones to make fire. If they rubbed two stones together, they could make sparks of[89] fire. Fire helped early people stay warm, cook food, and keep wild animals away.[103]

KEY NOTES

Tools

How did the earliest people use tools?

_____

_____

The Stone Age

The earliest people planted and stored food like corn, rice, and wheat.

Fast Facts

- Toe bones of the earliest people show that they spent a long time planting food.

- Farming let the earliest people build houses because they no longer had to search for food.

- Stone-Age people used plant roots to add color to paintings.

Food

Early people moved from place to place to hunt animals and find plants to eat. In winter, food was hard[21] to find. However, stone tools helped people dig holes to hide seeds from animals. Once people learned to grow plants, though, they did not have to go looking for food.[51]

Some of the first plants that people grew were grains such as corn, wheat, and rice. Then, people learned to[71] make flour by using stones to crush and grind grain. They also learned to store flour for winter, when plants[91] didn't grow. Growing and storing food helped early people feed themselves all year.[104]

KEY NOTES

Food
What kinds of food did early people eat?

_____

_____

The Stone Age

Tame sheep made life better for Stone-Age people.

Fast Facts

- Some scientists believe cats have been kept as pets since the Stone Age.

- The earliest cave paintings often show animals, such as bulls, horses, and deer.

- Stone-Age people used the skin of animals for clothing and shelter.

Animals

At first, Stone-Age people hunted animals for food. Over time, though, people found that animals could[18] be used in other ways, too. People began to tame the animals that we now call goats, cows, sheep, and dogs.[39] Goats and cows made milk that people used as food. People used the wool from sheep to keep warm. People[59] used dogs to herd other animals, like sheep. Dogs also kept people safe from wild animals.[75]

Once people learned to tame horses, their lives got even better. This is because horses could move people and things in less time and with less work.[102]

KEY NOTES

Animals

Why were animals important to people during the Stone Age?

_____

_____

The Stone Age

The Earliest People

1. Scientists don't know much about the earliest people because _____

    a. scientists can't read their writing.
    b. scientists haven't found their art or tools.
    c. the earliest people did not talk about how they lived.

2. How did early people use tools?

_____

_____

_____

3. The time long ago is called the Stone Age because people used stones _____

    a. to make tools.
    b. to make houses.
    c. to make drawings.

Tools

1. "Tools" is MAINLY about _____

    a. where people found tools.
    b. how tools helped early people.
    c. why tools were hard to use.

2. How did early people use stones and animal bones to make tools?

_____

_____

_____

3. How did fire help the earliest people?

_____

_____

_____

Food

1. Why did early people move from place to place?

    a. to find grains and flour

    b. to plant seeds

    c. to find food

2. How did growing plants help early people?

_____

_____

_____

3. Name two ways stone tools helped the earliest people to farm.

_____

_____

_____

Animals

1. Another good name for "Animals" is _____

    a. "Taming Horses."
    b. "Hunting Animals."
    c. "Animals and People."

2. How did horses change Stone-Age people's lives?

    a. Horses could be used for food.
    b. Horses could move people and things.
    c. Horses could hunt other animals.

3. Tell how Stone-Age people used two kinds of animals.

_____

_____

_____

earliest	scientists	stronger
winter	store	horses

1. Choose the word from the word box above that best matches each definition. Write the word on the line below.

A. _____ to keep things safe so they can be used later

B. _____ before anything else

C. _____ people who study things to learn about them

D. _____ standing for a longer time than something else

E. _____ large, strong animals with four legs and a tail

F. _____ the coldest season of the year

2. Fill in the blanks in the sentences below. Choose the word from the word box that completes each sentence.

A. Once they had enough food to _____, early people did not have to worry about being hungry.

B. A bridge made of steel is _____ than a bridge made of wood.

C. It is too cold to grow plants outside in the _____.

D. People sometimes use _____ for riding or for pulling carts.

E. The _____ time I will get up is 6:00 in the morning. I don't like to get up when it is dark.

F. Some _____ are looking for ways to help people get well more quickly.

The Stone Age

1. Use the idea web to help you remember what you read. In each box, write the main idea of that reading.

The Earliest People

_____

_____

_____

_____

Tools

_____

_____

_____

_____

The Stone Age

Food

_____

_____

_____

_____

Animals

_____

_____

_____

_____

2. Tell about two ways Stone-Age people made their lives better.

_____

_____

_____

_____

3. Tell about two ways life today is different from life in the Stone Age.

_____

_____

_____

_____

4. What can the bones, art, and tools of early people tell scientists about how they lived?

_____

_____

_____

_____

Realistic Fiction

Realistic fiction can be funny or sad.

Fast Facts

- More books of realistic fiction are sold than any other kinds of books for teens.

- Realistic fiction books can be picture books or chapter books.

- Some realistic fiction books for teens are known as "problem books."

What Is Realistic Fiction?

Realistic fiction tells stories about things that could really happen. The stories can be funny or sad. Realistic[22] stories are alike, though, in that they are set in the everyday world. In addition, the people speak and act the way real people do.[47]

The people and the things that happen in realistic fiction aren't real. However, realistic stories are about[64] problems that people face every day. Readers can learn new ideas and ways of doing things. They can come to[84] understand other people's lives and feelings. Realistic fiction can also give readers ideas about how to solve the problems they face in their own everyday lives.[110]

KEY NOTES

What Is Realistic Fiction?

How do the people in realistic fiction speak and act?

_____

_____

Realistic Fiction

Walter Dean Myers gets some of his ideas for stories from things that happened to him when he was a teen.

Fast Facts

- Walter Dean Myers started writing stories when he was in sixth grade.

- Myers has been given more than 25 awards.

- Myers says about writing, "This is something that I love to do."

Walter Dean Myers

Walter Dean Myers, who writes realistic fiction, has lived a life that is much like the lives of his characters.[23] Myers was two years old when his mother died. After that, he moved to New York City and spent a lot of time[46] on the streets. Some of Myers's ideas come from things that happened to him there.[61]

Myers creates many characters who are teens living in cities. Some have hard lives, but they often find ways[80] to make their lives better. His books have won many honors. Myers has been honored for writing about real[99] problems, but also for using his stories to help teens make their own lives better.[114]

KEY NOTES

Walter Dean Myers
What does Walter Dean Myers write about?

_____

_____

Realistic Fiction

The character Slam is a good basketball player who wants to join a pro team.

Fast Facts

- Walter Dean Myers was raised in Harlem, New York, where his book *Slam!* is set.

- Myers played basketball in high school, but he wasn't good enough to become a pro.

- *Slam!* shows that it takes more than basketball skills to be a success in life.

A Realistic Character

In a book by Walter Dean Myers, the main character is called Slam because he plays basketball so well. Slam[23] wants to join a pro team, but to do this, he must get better grades.[38]

Although a friend shows him how to take control of his schoolwork, Slam has other problems, too. He has to[58] learn how to get along with the other teens in his school. Slam also has to decide what to do when he sees one of[83] his friends doing something that is against the law. Slam decides that, if he really wants to reach his goals, he must take control of all parts of his life.[113]

KEY NOTES

A Realistic Character
What does Slam need to do to join a pro team?

_____

_____

Realistic Fiction

This book cover shows that the realistic story is set in the past.

Fast Facts

- Characters in historical fiction should speak the way people spoke at the time the story is set.

- Historical fiction has even been written about people who lived in caves thousands of years ago.

- A lot of realistic fiction is about problems teens face.

Reading Realistic Fiction

People enjoy reading different kinds of realistic fiction. Historical fiction is realistic fiction that is set[19] in the past. Writers of historical fiction might use real people, but create a story around them. They might also[39] use real events, but add characters they create. When they use real characters or events, writers of historical fiction must make sure their facts are right.[65]

Writers can also set realistic fiction in the present. This kind of realistic fiction may be about problems[83] people really face or events that really happen. Many people enjoy realistic fiction that is set in the[101] present because it helps them understand the world around them.[111]

KEY NOTES

Reading Realistic Fiction
What is historical fiction?

_____

_____

Realistic Fiction

What Is Realistic Fiction?

1. Another good name for "What Is Realistic Fiction?" is _____

   a. "Books Teens Like to Read."
   b. "Writing True Stories."
   c. "Fiction That Seems Real."

2. Why did the author write "Realistic Fiction"? _____

   a. to tell what books are realistic
   b. to tell how to write realistic fiction
   c. to tell what realistic fiction is like

3. What is realistic fiction?

_____

_____

_____

Walter Dean Myers

1. What does the word *characters* mean in this reading?

_____

_____

_____

2. This reading is MAINLY about _____

    a. why Myers writes books.
    b. the kinds of books Myers writes.
    c. the honors that Myers has received.

3. Explain your answer to question 2.

_____

_____

_____

A Realistic Character

1. In this reading, *taking control* means _____

    a. having the power to change things.
    b. listening carefully to others.
    c. doing better in schoolwork.

2. Tell about two problems that Slam faces.

_____

_____

_____

3. What does Slam learn? _____

    a. that playing basketball leads to success
    b. that playing basketball is hard work
    c. that it is not always easy to reach your goals

Reading Realistic Fiction

1. This reading is MAINLY about _____

    a. what historical fiction is.

    b. different kinds of realistic fiction.

    c. how to write realistic fiction about the present.

2. Tell about two kinds of realistic fiction.

_____

_____

_____

3. Why do writers of historical fiction have to know about the past?

_____

_____

_____

events	realistic	honors	fiction
decide	characters	historical	control

1. Choose the word from the word box above that best matches each definition. Write the word on the line below.

A. _____ awards given to someone who has done something special

B. _____ to make a choice about something

C. _____ people who are in stories

D. _____ things that happen

E. _____ something that seems like it could happen in real life

F. _____ writing that tells about made-up events

G. _____ to have power over something

H. _____ about the past

2. Fill in the blanks in the sentences below. Choose the word from the word box that completes each sentence.

A. Some important _____ in my life include making the team and getting a good grade in math.

B. Anna had to _____ whether to stay home or go to the store.

C. The _____ story showed me what life was like many years ago.

D. The book was very _____ because I felt like it was about my life.

E. She was given _____ for all of her work helping children.

F. I like to see the kinds of characters writers create when they write _____.

G. I see she can _____ her dog, because the dog walks right next to her.

H. The book had so many _____ I couldn't keep track of their names.

145

Realistic Fiction

1. Use the idea web to help you remember what you read. In each box, write the main idea of that reading.

What Is Realistic Fiction?

_____

_____

_____

_____

Walter Dean Myers

_____

_____

_____

_____

Realistic Fiction

A Realistic Character

_____

_____

_____

_____

Reading Realistic Fiction

_____

_____

_____

_____

2. Tell about the difference between realistic fiction and other kinds of writing.

_____

_____

_____

_____

3. Why do you think people write realistic fiction?

_____

_____

_____

_____

4. Tell about a realistic fiction book or story you have read. What made the characters or events seem real?

_____

_____

_____

_____

Word Play

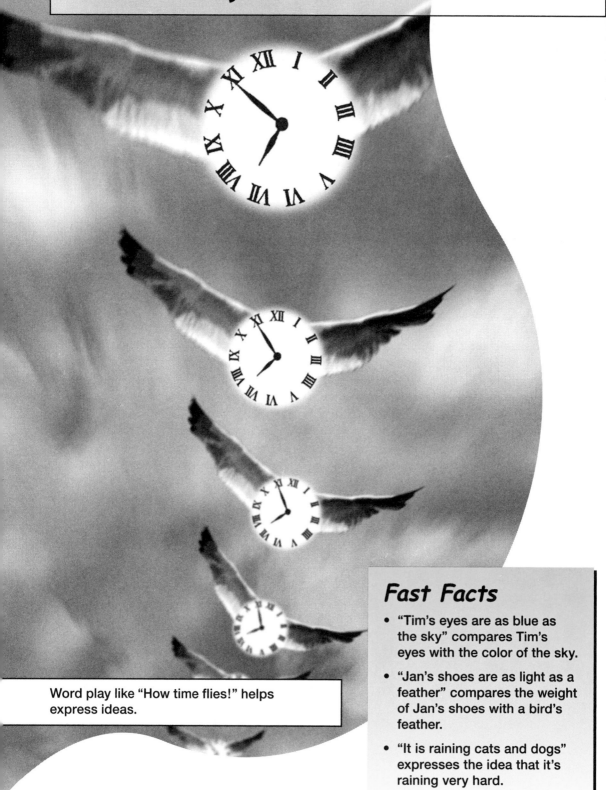

Word play like "How time flies!" helps express ideas.

Fast Facts

- "Tim's eyes are as blue as the sky" compares Tim's eyes with the color of the sky.

- "Jan's shoes are as light as a feather" compares the weight of Jan's shoes with a bird's feather.

- "It is raining cats and dogs" expresses the idea that it's raining very hard.

What Is Word Play?

"That's a cool shirt." You know what these words mean without thinking about them. You know that the[22] shirt is not really cold, but that the person likes the shirt. This is an example of word play, or words that are used in ways that are different from their real meaning.[55]

Word play can help you express your ideas. It can help you compare things that are not really alike. Word[75] play can also help you express how strongly you feel about something.[87]

It would be hard to compare things without word play. Word play can also help people bring pictures to mind, helping them see what others are saying.[114]

KEY NOTES

What Is Word Play?
How can word play help you express your ideas?

_____

_____

Word Play

Finding CDs is "like looking for a needle in a haystack."

Fast Facts

- Here is a comparison using *like:* "Lou looks like a giant in that picture."

- Some people use *is* to compare things: "Love is sunshine."

- You make comparisons when you shop, too, noting how two shirts are alike.

Comparisons

Comparison is one type of word play. When people make a comparison, they say something is like[18] something else. Sometimes writers use the words *like* or *as* to compare two things. For example, "Mary is as busy as a bee" is a comparison.[44]

To understand this comparison, picture how a bee moves—it flies quickly from one place to another. Now,[62] think about how Mary might be like a bee. She must move quickly. The purpose of this comparison is to help you see how Mary moves.[88]

The purpose of comparisons, like "busy as a bee," is to make your ideas clear to others. Comparisons help people draw pictures in their mind.[113]

KEY NOTES
Comparisons
What is a comparison?
_____
_____

Word Play

Exaggeration makes words sound funny.

Fast Facts

- The word *exaggerate* comes from Latin words meaning "to pile up high."

- Exaggerations are often used to make people laugh.

- For example, "When I climb the ropes in gym, I feel like I'm climbing to the sky," is an exaggeration.

Exaggerations

Sometimes a comparison is an exaggeration. In this type of word play, something is described as being bigger[19] than it really is. Here is an example: "My cat is as big as a house!" We know that this cannot be true because[43] no cat can be as big as a house. Yet, we understand the idea because it makes a strong picture in our mind. The[67] speaker has had a stronger effect than if he or she had simply said, "My cat is very, very big."[87]

People use exaggeration for effect. They want their words to sound important or funny. Exaggerations also can be used to make a strong point about something.[113]

KEY NOTES

Exaggerations
What is an exaggeration?

_____

_____

Word Play

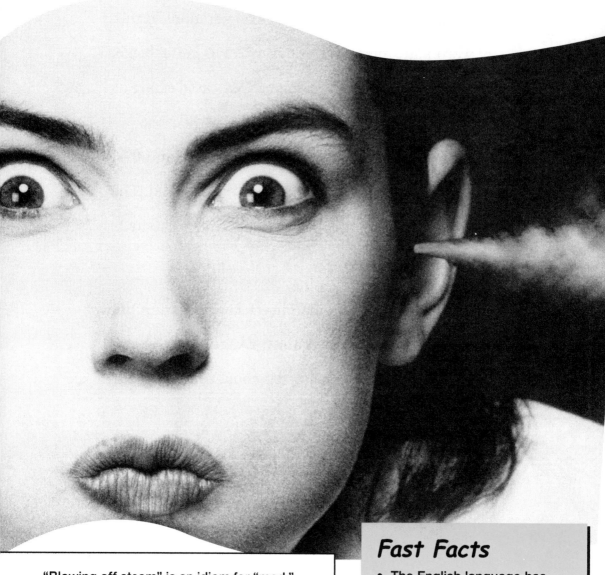

"Blowing off steam" is an idiom for "mad."

Fast Facts

- The English language has thousands of idioms.

- New idioms are created every day.

- In English, people "take a walk." However, in Spanish they "give a walk."

Idioms

Another kind of word play is called an idiom. An idiom is a group of words that can't be understood from[22] each word's literal, or word for word, meaning. Here is an example: "Tom got the story straight from the horse's[42] mouth." The literal meaning of this example is that a horse told Tom the story. However, this idiom really[61] means that Tom learned about something that happened from someone who was there.[74]

Idioms are sometimes hard for people from another country to understand. They know the literal meaning of[91] each word, but the sentence doesn't make sense. This can make it hard to guess at what the speaker is saying.[112]

KEY NOTES
Idioms
What is an idiom?
_____
_____

Word Play

What Is Word Play?

1. What is word play?

    a. using words in ways different from their real meanings
    b. using words with their real meanings.
    c. using words to learn how to play games or sports

2. Name two ways you can use word play.

_____

_____

_____

3. Why is "That's a cool shirt" an example of word play?

_____

_____

_____

Comparisons

1. "Comparisons" is MAINLY about _____

    a. how word play was first used.
    b. why word play compares things that are not alike.
    c. how people help others understand them.

2. What does *purpose* mean in this reading?

    a. why you should compare things
    b. the reason to do something
    c. how one thing is like another

3. Why might you want to make a comparison?

_____

_____

_____

Exaggerations

1. Which words BEST describe an exaggeration?

    a. a way of talking in which people use their hands
    b. something that is said to be much larger than it really is
    c. an important point made with big words

2. How are comparisons and exaggerations alike?

_____

_____

_____

3. What are two reasons people use exaggeration?

_____

_____

_____

Idioms

1. Another good name for "Idioms" is _____

    a. "What Do You Mean?"

    b. "Pictures in Your Mind."

    c. "Old and Strange Sayings."

2. Which answer choice means about the same as *literal*?

    a. from a book

    b. exact

    c. incorrect

3. Why is it hard to guess at the meaning of an idiom?

_____

_____

_____

express	compare	comparison	purpose
exaggeration	effect	idiom	literal

1. Choose the word from the word box above that best matches each definition. Write the word on the line below.

A. _____ to show a person's feelings or thoughts

B. _____ something someone plans to do

C. _____ something that is said to be greater than it really is

D. _____ a result

E. _____ a group of words that can't be understood from each word's usual meaning

F. _____ to show how two things are alike

G. _____ taking words at their usual meaning

H. _____ showing how two things are like one another

2. Fill in the blanks in the sentences below. Choose the word from the word box that completes each sentence.

A. A _____ of the two teams showed that our team was stronger.

B. Before he buys a bike, Jim likes to _____ the two best models.

C. "Take a walk" is an example of an English _____.

D. The _____ of staying up too late was that Carol could not work the next day.

E. Dancers _____ themselves by moving in certain ways.

F. The _____ meaning of "to fly off the handle" is "to jump off a pan."

G. Even if you are very hungry, it is an _____ to say that you can eat a horse.

H. The _____ of this meeting is to figure out how to solve the problem.

Word Play

1. Use the idea web to help you remember what you read. In each box, write the main idea of that reading.

What Is Word Play?

_____

_____

_____

_____

Comparisons

_____

_____

_____

_____

Word Play

Exaggerations

_____

_____

_____

_____

Idioms

_____

_____

_____

_____

2. What is the same about all of these kinds of word play?

_____

_____

_____

_____

3. Name two ways you can use word play in everyday speech.

_____

_____

_____

_____

4. Is "Word Play" a good title for these readings? Why or why not?

_____

_____

_____

_____

Real-World Reading

Labels tell something about the food we eat.

Fast Facts

- Most labels use only a few words so you can quickly find what you need to know.

- Road signs tell you important information.

- Money in this country has the words *United States of America* to show where it was made.

Words All Around You

Words are all around you. The clothes you wear have words on their labels. There are labels on the boxes of [25] food you eat. On your way to school, signs tell you to stop or to go. When you need to buy something, the words on [50] money tell you and the store how much money you have. The words also tell you something about your country. [70] Signs and labels tell you about games you watch or play, too. [82]

Signs and labels are words you read every day. You may not read them in a book, but they are words that help you get around in the world. [111]

KEY NOTES
Words All Around You
What words do you see around you every day?
_____
_____

Real-World Reading

Read the words and pictures in directions when you cook.

Fast Facts

- The first cake mix was made in the 1940s.

- People eat certain cakes on certain days, such as wedding cakes and birthday cakes.

- Cookbooks have directions for making many different foods.

Making a Cake

You want something to eat, so you look at what you have. You find a box of cake mix, but you must read the[27] directions on the box before you start making the cake. Directions tell you how to make the cake. Sometimes[46] there are pictures with the directions. The pictures might be of eggs, milk, or oil. You might have to measure 1 cup of milk or oil.[72]

After you have measured the things you need, you look for time clue words, like *first* and *next*. These words[92] will help you follow the directions in the right order. If you follow the directions, your cake will come out right.[113]

KEY NOTES
Making a Cake
What are directions?
_____
_____

Real-World Reading

A menu lists the foods the restaurant sells.

Eating Out

Signs are very important in restaurants. The name of the restaurant is often written on a sign outside.[20] Inside, you can read the menu, which lists the foods the restaurant sells. Some menus have pictures with labels[39] that show you how the food looks. After you eat, signs tell you where to throw things out.[57]

Cities around the world have many kinds of restaurants. People around the world use different words[73] for foods, too. Yet, at some restaurants, you will still be able to read the sign outside and the menu. Although[94] there may be some different foods in other countries, you will still see—and read about—foods you know.[113]

KEY NOTES

Eating Out
What kinds of things can you read in restaurants?

_____

_____

Real-World Reading

Numbers and logos on shirts help people watch a game.

Fast Facts

- You can read the signs players make with their hands, like "T" for "time out."

- Many game balls, shirts, hats, and other things have team logos.

- Games on TV have score signs that tell who is winning.

Watching a Game

During a great game, things can happen fast. It can be hard to find out important things, like who scored a[24] point. Everyday words can help people figure out what happened. For example, one side of a score sign might[43] show points for "Home." The other side might show points for "Away."[55]

The players might also wear words. Sometimes the names and numbers of the players are written on their[73] backs. Players' shirts might also have a team name or a logo, like a bird. Logos can work like signs, helping[94] people read who are far away. They can help people learn which team scored the point.[110]

KEY NOTES

Watching a Game
What can you read when you watch a game?

_____

_____

Real-World Reading

Words All Around You

1. "Words All Around You" is MAINLY about _____

    a. words you read every day.
    b. words you read in books.
    c. words that are on money.

2. How do labels and signs help people?

_____

_____

_____

3. Name three places you see words in the real world.

_____

_____

_____

Making a Cake

1. Another good name for "Making a Cake" is _____

    a. "After School Snacks."
    b. "Reading Directions."
    c. "Measuring Things."

2. In this reading, to *measure* means _____

    a. to mix things together.
    b. to split something into even parts.
    c. to find the right amount of something.

3. Why should you look for time clue words when you make something?

_____

_____

_____

Eating Out

1. What is a menu?

    a. a box for taking food home
    b. a list of foods
    c. a sign with the restaurant's name

2. Where are two places that you can find signs in restaurants?

_____

_____

_____

3. What is this reading MAINLY about?

_____

_____

_____

Watching a Game

1. Another good name for "Watching a Game" is _____

    a. "Reading at the Game."
    b. "Home and Away Games."
    c. "Keeping Score."

2. What is a logo?

    a. a picture that shows teams from far away
    b. a picture of a bird
    c. a picture that stands for the name of something

3. How do everyday words help people watch a game?

_____

_____

_____

labels	signs	directions	measure
restaurant	menu	score	logo

1. Choose the word from the word box above that best matches each definition. Write the word on the line below.

A. _____ to make points in a game

B. _____ tags that show what something is or what's in it

C. _____ a picture that stands for the name of something

D. _____ to find the right amount of something

E. _____ step-by-step plans for doing something

F. _____ boards with words that tell you what to do

G. _____ a place where people can buy and eat food

H. _____ a list of foods you can get at a restaurant

2. Fill in the blanks in the sentences below. Choose the word from the word box that completes each sentence.

A. I need _____ that tell me how to fix my radio.

B. The _____ on the street told me where to park the car.

C. My favorite _____ makes the best pizza I've ever had.

D. Did Tom _____ the point that won the game?

E. Please _____ the flour so we can make the cake.

F. Dena read the _____ carefully before she chose what to eat.

G. My shirt has my team's _____ on it. It is a picture of an arrow.

H. Sam reads food _____ to know what is in it.

Real-World Reading

1. Use the idea web to help you remember what you read. In each box, write the main idea of that reading.

Words All Around You

_____

_____

_____

_____

Making a Cake

_____

_____

_____

_____

Real-World Reading

Eating Out

_____

_____

_____

_____

Watching a Game

_____

_____

_____

_____

2. What is real-world reading?

_____

_____

_____

_____

3. In what two ways are signs and logos alike?

_____

_____

_____

_____

4. Tell about two kinds of real-world reading you do every day.

_____

_____

_____

_____

Acknowledgments

Photo Credits

Cover photos: (top) BananaStock/Punchstock; (bottom, L-R) Stockbyte Silver/Getty Images; Comstock Images/Punchstock; Digital Vision/ Punchstock; Dave Bartruff/Digital Vision/Getty Images; **Page:** 8 Vince Cavataio/PacificStock. com; 10 Pearson Learning Photo Studio; 12 © David Young-Wolff/PhotoEdit Inc.; 14 © Michael Newman/PhotoEdit; 22 European Southern Observatory/Photo Researchers, Inc.; 24 A. Morton/Photo Researchers, Inc.; 26 Chris Butler/Photo Researchers, Inc.; 28 D. Nunuk/ Photo Researchers, Inc.; 36 Michael Dalton/ Fundamental Photographs, NYC; 38 © Robert Brenner/PhotoEdit Inc.; 40 © Image Source/ Corbis. All Rights Reserved.; 42 © David Young-Wolff/PhotoEdit; 50 © Ted Spiegel/Corbis; 52 © Bruce Connolly/Corbis; 54 © Tria Giovan/Corbis; 56 © Royalty-Free/Corbis; 64 Scala/Art Resource, NY; 66 © 2007 The Munch Museum/The Munch-Ellingsen Group/Artists Rights Society (ARS), NY; 68 Art Resource, NY; 70 © National Gallery Collection; By kind permission of the Trustees of the National Gallery, London/Corbis; 78 © Phil Borden/PhotoEdit; 80 Jeff Haynes/ AFP/Getty Images; 82 Michael Mauney/Stone Allstock/Getty Images; 84 Getty Images, Inc.; 92 U.S. Dept. of Agriculture; 94 © Neal Preston/ Corbis. All Rights Reserved.; 96 National Air and Space Museum, Smithsonian Institution; 98 Charles Drew Papers. Moorland-Spingarn Research Center, Howard University; 106 Digital Vision/Getty Images; 108 © David Young-Wolff/ PhotoEdit; 110 © Comstock/Corbis; 112 Spencer Grant/Photo Researchers, Inc.; 120 © David Muench/SuperStock, Inc.; 122 Comstock/Jupiter Images; 124 Wesley Hitt/Mira.com; 126 © Geoff Simpson/Nature Picture Library; 134 © George Doyle/Stockbyte/Punchstock; 136 Miriam Berkley; 138 © Robert Brenner/PhotoEdit; 140 Derek James; 148 © Novastock/age fotostock; 150 Howard Grey/Stone/Getty Images; 152 © Jiang Jin/SuperStock; 154 David Waldorf/Taxi/Getty Images; 162 © David Young-Wolff/PhotoEdit Inc.; 164 © David Young-Wolff/PhotoEdit; 166 Pearson Ed. Corp. Digital Archive; 168 © Rudi Von Briel/PhotoEdit

Text Credits

- *The Mona Lisa (La Gioconda).* 1503-06. Leonardo da Vinci (1452-1519). Location: The Louvre, Paris, France.
- *The Scream* by Edvard Munch (1863-1944). Location: National Gallery, Oslo, Norway.
- *Vase with Fourteen Sunflowers.* 1889. Vincent van Gogh (1853-1890). Location: Van Gogh Museum, Amsterdam, The Netherlands.
- *The Water-Lily Pond.* 1899. Claude Monet (1840-1926). Location: Pushkin Museum of Fine Arts, Moscow.
- CowParade® is a registered trademark of CowParade Holdings Corporation. Copyright © CowParade Holdings Corporation. All rights reserved.
- *Slam!* Copyright © 1996 by Walter Dean Myers. All rights reserved. Published by Scholastic Inc.
- *The Gates, Central Park, New York, 1979-2005.* Copyright © Christo.

Staff Credits

Members of the AMP™ QReads™ team: Melania Benzinger, Karen Blonigen, Carol Bowling, Michelle Carlson, Kazuko Collins, Nancy Condon, Barbara Drewlo, Sue Gulsvig, Daren Hastings, Laura Henrichsen, Ruby Hogen-Chin, Julie Johnston, Mary Kaye Kuzma, Julie Maas, Daniel Milowski, Carrie O'Connor, Julie Theisen, Mary Verrill, Mike Vineski, Charmaine Whitman